Boxcar Baby

This is a compilation of hilarious episodes that occurred during my childhood.

GEORGE SOLANO

ISBN 979-8-89243-587-1 (paperback)
ISBN 979-8-89243-588-8 (digital)

Library of Congress TXU1-236-277

Copyright © 2024 by George Solano

All rights reserved. No part of this publication may be reproduced, distributed, or transmitted in any form or by any means, including photocopying, recording, or other electronic or mechanical methods without the prior written permission of the publisher. For permission requests, solicit the publisher via the address below.

Christian Faith Publishing
832 Park Avenue
Meadville, PA 16335
www.christianfaithpublishing.com

Printed in the United States of America

To Rhonda, Floyd, Paul, and Cora
For only through their consistent persistence was I
challenged to write this portion of my life.

Acknowledgments

Special acknowledgement goes to my father and mother, whom I love dearly for correcting me each time on the rough road to leading a good life.

Condolence

My sincere condolences to my wife, Toni, for now she is saddled with the original boxcar baby.

Introduction

What seems to be many generations ago and yet less than half a century, time, though never changing but combined with circumstances. It seems as if that period in my life was so completely different—so in touch with the world and yet so remote, as if everything I am about to write happened on a different world, in some other universe.

Even now, it is hard to believe that the world existed before television and indoor toilets. How did people live and survive in those olden days just after World War II? How my parents coped with the economy, religion, and politics, I cannot say, since I was too young to know. Besides, it was a time when children were seen and not heard, and psychology was applied at the right end.

A person's imagination really has to be strong to imagine a time when two cents could buy almost a quarter pound of jelly beans or three pieces of bubble gum. Also, a time when one could buy Howdy Doody cupcakes and an ice cream bar for only ten cents. Oh, how parents must wish for those days when coffee was thirty cents a pound, bread was twelve cents a loaf, potatoes were a dollar for fifty pounds, and milk was twenty-nine cents a quart.

Though television had been invented, it had yet to cross the Mississippi. For us, way out west in the Indian country of Colorado, television seemed to be something out of Jules Verne; there was no way to see it, and one could not imagine full-grown people in a little box in the living room. But our imagination soared each Saturday listening to "Only the Shadow Knows," "Inner Sanctum," "Mr. and Mrs. North," "The Lone Ranger," "Amos and Andy," and "Sparky," to mention only a few of the radio programs. One would find the entire family gathered around the radio, each person sitting on the edge of their seat, leaning forward, waiting on each word as if trying to capture it before it left the speaker.

It was a time when your neighbor was a neighbor, and your neighbor was anyone within three blocks, known not only by the children but also by the parents, a time when neighbors gathered for events on holidays and visited on Sundays. Oh yes, a time when one did not try to keep up with the Joneses because they were just the same as you. A time when newspapers were filled with more good news than bad, highways were made of cement instead of asphalt, and the most dependable item you could buy was made in America, not Japan.

What a wonderful time it was, for not a day went by without going to the house in back to scan through the Sears and Roebuck or Montgomery Ward catalogs, which never seemed to run out, giving everyone the opportunity to dream as they sat on the throne in what always seemed to be the red outhouse. A time so long ago, and yet it seems as if I was there just yesterday, in that world long gone. Though perhaps not in exact sequence, listed here are but a few of my memorable moments, in hopes of letting you have some idea of my life, until I learned how it came to be that I was born in a boxcar.

Portland

Returning from the big city of Florence, nine miles away, one could enter Portland, Colorado, traveling east toward Pueblo on the only highway going through the three-block town. After coming down the winding road and rounding the curve, you pass over the creek, and just before you reach the town limits on the right side, you pass the rainbow inn, also known as Chow's or Rocchio's, the only tavern within nine miles. As you reach the town limits, the road slopes downward, and you find yourself flanked on the left by the railroad tracks, which were about four feet higher than the road, and on the right by the lazy L-shaped hill, which must have been three hundred feet high.

There, at the base of the hill, began the town of Portland, which probably never had over one thousand residents, even when the town was at its largest during the two years after World War II had ended. The row of houses erected by the cement plant for its superintendents began near the base of the hill, set back off the road about fifteen feet. Each house, being exactly like the next, resembled a rectangle with an inverted V roof of tar shingles. The porch in front extended the full width of the house, cemented one-fourth of the way up from the foundation between four square posts, except for the entrance located at the center. Steps came down from the porch to meet the walkway, which passed a cottonwood tree on the left side and joined the sidewalk about ten feet to the front. Directly in front of each walkway and between the street and sidewalk stood the lampposts, which were about a foot thick and in the form of a letter T, with a round bulb hanging from each end of the crossbar, one suspended over the street and the other over the sidewalk. Every house, tree, and lamppost was in a perfect line to the end of the second block, where the superintendents' houses ended. The lampposts continued down and in front of the cement plant until the road turned left, going over the river on its way to Pueblo.

At the end of the line of superintendents' houses, there was an empty lot of well-manicured lawn about forty feet wide, and next to it was Wilbar's Mercantile, the only store in town. Inside, one could find every type of candy, ice cream, vegetables, meat, canned and dry goods, dress and work clothing, plus material and all sewing needs, and they even had a section carrying all types of shoes, including shoes with steel toes required for work at the plant. The post office, which may have had seven hundred boxes, was located in the same building as the store. The entrance to the post office was on the left side as you faced south from the road and about three feet from the back of the store, and we had box number 101. But what I will never forget is that in the shoe section, Mr. Wilbar kept two rabbits, each about three feet tall, one pink and the other white.

Directly behind the store and post office was a cement parking lot extending the length of the building and about fifty feet wide. At the edge of the parking lot, facing the back of the store, was the small emergency hospital and clinic, which had twelve beds and an operating room. The one and only doctor, a short, stocky man in his late fifties with bushy eyebrows and a full head of white hair, handled all the medical needs of every family in town and gave physicals to all the men who worked at the plant. Dr. Davis always had two things: a smile for each person and candy for every child. He was more than a doctor to each person in town and even made house calls at any hour, day or night, even though the town was so small. His concern for each patient equaled that of family members and a more joyful person one could not find.

To the left side of the clinic was a road that ran in front of the post office and connected with the road which ran in front of our house and also with the main highway. Across the road from the clinic was the firehouse, which was five feet wide and ten feet high at the highest point. Inside was a hand-pulled cart made with a spool on which the fire hose was wrapped around, and it was suspended between two three-foot-high iron wheels, with the handle connecting at the axle.

Across the parking lot and post office were three big two-story mansions with great big circular columns going around three sides of the house. So big, beautiful, and impressive were they that one could almost smell richness. Each house had five bedrooms, with a maid's room downstairs, plus a great big reception, living and dining rooms, and a giant kitchen. The president of the company lived in the house across from the post office, and behind his house was the vice president's house. Across the parking lot and next to the president's house was the last mansion, and that was Dr. Davis's house.

Just past the vice president's house was a big conveyor belt that ran from the plant, high above the road and tracks, and over the river from where the cement rock was brought into the plant. That conveyor belt was almost as long as the town. As you looked at the plant from the road, up about two hundred feet, you would see an opening about two and a half feet square in the tin, and that is where my dad worked. Many times, as I walked home from school, which was about three blocks behind and to the left of the cement plant, I could look up and we would wave at each other.

About a block past the conveyor belt and almost in front of the cement plant's main office, on the left side of the road, was the railroad station where the train stopped five times a week. From there, the tracks crossed the river and went under the road bridge as they made their way to Pueblo.

The church in town was located at the end of the first block as you entered the town from Florence. There, each Sunday, the Protestant minister held services at nine o'clock, and a priest would come from the Holy Cross Abbey in Canon City, bringing a nun to hold catechism at ten, with Mass at eleven. The church itself was not fancy but had a big statue above the double doors as you entered and could hold about one hundred people.

On the other side of the alley and directly behind the church was the only gas station and garage. There, in the center, two blocks behind the church and the company houses, and also behind the firehouse and south to the base of the hill, was where all the new people who came to town built houses of wood and tin. Most of these houses did not last more than six years after the war was over because many lost their jobs and went to work in the coal mines near Florence, or at the steel mill in Pueblo.

The only other houses that were permanent besides the company-built homes were my uncle's and ours, both of which were made of bricks. My uncle Flavio's house was across the street and almost directly behind the garage, and it was also rectangular with an inverted V roof of tin. Behind his house, he had a chicken coop which was almost half as big as his house. To the left of his house was his garage, and in the center between the house and garage was a lonely water faucet that came up out of the ground about three feet high. Next to the garage was an empty field that never had any houses built on it.

To the left of the empty field and even with my uncle's house was our house. It was a perfect square, about forty feet each way, and the roof went up from all sides almost to a point at the center, and it was covered with shingles instead of tin. At the top of the roof in the center, it was flat, with just enough room for the chimney, which went on up about three feet. In fact, our house was the only one of its kind in town.

Beginning at the right side of the house, as you faced it from the street, was a white picket fence made of quarter-inch strips of wood about two inches wide and about three feet high at the point, extending about ten feet to the front of the house along the walkway, with a gate right in the middle made of two-by-fours with the same narrow pieces of wood nailed to the street side of the two-by-fours, which was held in place by four-by-fours. As you swung the gate inward going to the front door, you first came to the porch, which came out of the house for about five feet and was centered on the house. The porch was about ten feet long and was held up by four beams, with a railing made of one-inch square boards about three feet high, with a two-by-four on top of the beams. There, on the right-hand side of the porch, was a long wooden swing almost the width of the porch, held up by chains, two on each side, which came down from the roof and attached to the front and back of the armrests.

Entering the house as the door swung inward to the right, you would see the potbelly stove, which, along with the wood and coal stove in the kitchen, heated the entire house. To the right was the door to Mom and Dad's bedroom, and to the left was the couch, which was also made into a bed where my sister Ipa slept. A window was behind the couch, which almost went to the corner where the radio was on a small table. On the left, centered between the corner and the entrance to the kitchen, was a window, in front of which was the baby crib. Right next to the kitchen entrance and about three feet from the potbelly stove was Dad's lounge chair with his metal ashtray stand next to it. Every wall in the house was papered, and the ceiling was about ten feet high. The ceilings were painted white, as were the window frames. The house itself was divided into fourths, as each room measured almost twenty feet square. Entering the kitchen, there was the table, which was pushed up against the wall and under the window. Next to the table was the pantry, which was behind the water faucets and sink, which connected to the wall even with the back window frame. The back window was about two feet from the back door, and if a line were drawn, the back and front doors were in a straight line. Across the kitchen table was the wood and coal stove. And to the right of it, about six feet high on the wall, was the round kitchen clock.

Just before you went out the back door, there was a door on the right, and that is where my bedroom was. In there, I had a big round dining room table, a big china cabinet, the Maytag washing machine, and my bed, where my brother Ronnie and I slept.

Going out the back door and to the right was a sandbox, and about twenty feet behind the house on the same side as the sandbox were the rabbit pens. Behind the rabbit pens, about ten feet, was the chicken coop with a fence of chicken wire as high as the coop and about twelve feet square to the front of it. In front of the chicken yard was the woodpile, and about ten feet behind and to the left of it was the little coal shed, which was next to a house that was made of what once was a garage, and Doña Feliz, a neighbor who later became our boarder, lived in the little two-room house. On the left of her house was the garage, which was about half as high as her house, with a tin roof slanting from the front to the back. About five feet to the left of the garage was the outhouse, about four feet wide each way and about eight feet high, and its roof was of tin and almost flat, with a round chimney pipe at the far left corner. Across the chicken coop and rabbit pens and in front of the garage was another house where our cousins lived. Between their house and the street was where Dad always made his garden each summer.

To the left of our yard was a big field where a few houses were built, and near the base of the hill was a giant cottonwood tree, almost half as high as the hill. On that field, about one hundred feet from our yard, right next to the street, was a long row of garages used by the superintendents of the cement plant. At the end of the row of about twenty garages is where the street connected with the street that went in front of Dr. Davis's house.

The most exciting thing in town for us kids was to wait and watch for the steam locomotive to pass by with its whistle blowing and the bell clanging loudly as it went by so fast, leaving a trail of white smoke behind but taking each of us to distant places as we throttled the engine in our imagination.

This was Portland as I remember it shortly after the war had ended and where life began to unfold what it had in store for me.

Early Spring

It may have been in early spring when I was almost six, and all of us kids in the neighborhood were out at the playground in front of my house just having fun. We began to argue as to who was born in the strangest place because Charlie's brother had been born in their car on the way to the hospital on top of the bridge that crosses over the railroad tracks before you enter Rainbow Park on the way to Florence, the day before. Everyone started in with all kinds of different places, and oh, I was just waiting for my turn because the night before, when company from Pueblo was over, I had found out and was so proud. My turn finally came, and I said to all of them, "Shucks, that's nothing. I was born in a boxcar." Needless to say, I had been born in the strangest place. The news spread so fast that soon Mom found out, and for some unknown reason, which I could not for the life of me understand at the time, Mom exploded when she found out that I had told all the kids in town that I had been born in a boxcar. I can still remember what a deep shade of red my bottom carried for a few days. I guess simply because that was the first spanking I can remember, and that is the one you seem to remember better than all the others.

I guess I should explain it the way Dad explained it to me that evening when he came home from work. He said, "Son, Mom tells me that you know where you were born."

I answered, "Yes."

He continued, "Well, let me tell you how it came to be that you were born in a boxcar."

I knew then I was right because Dad had just said so, and now, I was going to find out all about it. I got down on the floor in front of Dad, lying on my stomach, my hands propping up my head, and my knees bent with my feet up in the air.

About that time, Mom came into the room with some coffee for Dad and a glass of goat milk for me. As Dad placed the coffee on the table next to his chair, I knew then exactly what Mom was going to say, and sure enough, "George, it's time for bed." I got so mad that I started to kick the floor. Then Dad reached forward and very gently swatted me one, and on top of what Mom had done, I knew better than to try and throw a tantrum because Dad was home. So I sat up, began to drink my milk, and just knew that I would have to wait until tomorrow, which was going to be Sunday and since Dad didn't have to work, I would have all day to find out how it came to be that I was born in a boxcar.

I finished drinking my milk, and Dad got out of his chair, bending over and picking me up, and throwing me into the air. I sure enjoyed it every time he did that. He carried me into my bedroom, and as he lowered me into my bed, a grin came to his face as he said, "Now stop sticking out that lower lip, and don't worry, Daddy will tell you all about it after Mass tomorrow." I was so happy and anxious because each Sunday Dad was off, and I could be with him all day. I could hardly wait for him to tell me about the boxcar and other stories as we did different things together all day.

Louder than a Cannon

Not knowing what time it was, since I could not tell time, I looked at the clock in the kitchen and saw the big hand pointing toward the chimney. I remembered how every Sunday, when the big hand was in the same place, Dad would look at the clock and always say, "We better hurry. It's ten till nine."

I walked into the living room where Fabbie was, and then very quietly, I passed by my big sister's bed to open the door to Mom and Dad's bedroom. I remember thinking about Ipa: that's what I always called my big sister because it was easier to say, and besides, Mary was a name for a really nice person, since Jesus's mother's name was Mary, and my sister was always picking on me. She would always stop me from waking up Mom and Dad and then stand there and yell and scream at me, not thinking that she always woke them up with all her screaming and yelling.

I had just finished opening the door all the way when Fabbie started to laugh a lot, so I walked over to her and told her to shush. She sat down behind her bars in the baby crib, holding on to two of them. Just then, I got the idea of running from the baby crib to Dad's bedroom and jumping on his bed. This way, if Ipa should wake up, she would not be able to stop me. I took off in a dead run, got past Ipa, through the door, and up into the air I went and down I came, dead center, right on top of Dad's chest.

Dad's eyes opened so wide as he gasped for air, as we continued to fall to the floor with a great big bang, for the bed had busted. The bang we made when we hit the floor was so loud it seemed like a cannon had gone off in the house. Ipa jumped out of bed, Fabbie started crying, and Dad, still trying to catch his breath, looked over at Mom, whose eyes were still so big with surprise, and said, "The baby's crying."

As I started in, "Daddy, you have to get up. Today is Sunday, and we will miss Mass if you don't hurry." Dad looked at his watch as Mom got up, and then I found out there was a louder sound than a cannon as Dad turned me over.

Besides, at that age, how was I to know that the little hand had to be next to the nine instead of near the five?

Education

"We'd better hurry. It's ten till nine," Dad said as Mom came out of the bedroom, all set to go. So out the door, we went, through the little gate, turning left. And, as usual, up the street about half a block, we could see my aunt waving her hands, trying to get us to hurry. You would think that by now, after all these years, she would quit getting so excited each Sunday morning. After all, we had yet to be late. Besides, the priest had never been on time yet and was usually fifteen to thirty minutes late. But I must admit, we never stayed longer than an hour. I often wondered what would happen if he were an hour late, just simply to see if he would say no Mass that day. But with my luck, he would go ahead and say Mass, and two hours would be shot.

My aunt was still waving her arms faster and faster as we walked past the big empty field full of weeds and grasshoppers between their house and ours. Mom was always saying there were rattlesnakes in there, but I never found one.

Well, my aunt finally stopped waving her hands as we all started off to church, and we made it with time to spare since the priest was ten minutes late. Oh, how happy I was when he came in because then we could stand up, for I still remembered and felt what had happened so early that morning. Finally, Mass was over, and now the day was all mine to be with Dad. We got home and had pancakes for breakfast, as usual on Sunday, and as Mom did the dishes, Dad and I went out in the yard.

As Dad chopped wood for the stove, I began taking it in a few sticks at a time and dumped them into the big wooden box by the stove. While I was still busy carrying the wood in, Dad fed the rabbits and chickens and was now taking out the 1932 (four-door) Buick, nicknamed the Ambulance. Oh, what a car that was, so big, black, and shiny. I finished taking the wood in, and Mom had me change clothes and wash again, as Dad brought the Buick beside the house, honking the horn, which made a sound like "too-too-loot-ta, too-too-loot-ta."

All dressed up and ready to go for a ride, we climbed aboard and went bumpety-bump over the dirt road until we came around the clinic and got on the cement road. Oh, how smooth the road was, except for the *thump, thump, thump* every so many feet. We went around another corner and down in front of the big cement plant, as Dad slowed down to show me exactly where he worked. But all I can remember is how where he worked must have been at least ten stories high. At least that is what it seemed at the time. After we passed the cement plant, we turned to the right and headed across the railroad tracks, over another dirt road, which went in front of the school that Ipa went to.

Just before we got to the last track, a train blew its whistle, and Dad came to a complete stop so fast that I flew off the seat. While we sat waiting for the train to pass, I asked Dad if I had to go to school when it started again. Before Dad had a chance to say anything, Mom answered, "Yes."

"That's right, son," Dad said, "because I don't want you to grow up not knowing how to read, write, or count. I want you to have what I did not have: an education."

Then Mom said, "You don't want Daddy to go to jail, do you?"

I naturally answered, "No."

As Mom explained, "If you don't go to school, the police will put Daddy in jail." As the train neared the end, I asked Dad if he had gone to school.

As he maneuvered the car to get it in motion again, he began to answer, "Not really," he stated, "because when he was my age, his dad couldn't afford to send him to school. There was no school in his town, and it was too expensive for him to go to the big city school. But when he was about eleven, his town finally had a school and a schoolteacher who taught all the grades. Most everyone had to start in the first grade because they had never been to school."

So when school started, he and four or five others who were his age would sit in the back of the classroom and try to pay attention as they looked out the window. Soon the teacher would lose her patience and holler at them that if they were learning so much by looking outside, perhaps they would learn more if they were outside looking in. In a flash, out the window, they would go. And always, the class would leave their desks, and out the windows, they would come. Sure enough, the teacher would run outside, and before she could catch anyone, most everyone would be back inside except for him, who always helped his sister Amalia back inside. Into the corner with the dunce hat, he would go for a short while, after which he was allowed to return to his desk. Then he would begin making spit wads, and each time the teacher turned around to face the blackboard, he would throw one to see how close he could get without hitting her and have the spit wad stick to the blackboard. Soon everyone in the class was doing it, and the teacher became madder and madder, until one time she turned around and spun back very quickly, just as Amalia had thrown a big spit wad, which landed smack dab between her eyes with a great big splash. They laughed and laughed as her face turned red in anger. He immediately went to Amalia's defense as the teacher called her forward. He told the teacher not to pick on his sister and that it was he who had thrown the spit wad. The teacher was so mad as she said she knew who had thrown it, but if he was dumb enough to come forward and accept punishment for his sister, to come forward.

Before leaving his sister's side, he complimented her on her good aim and hesitantly walked forward as the teacher withdrew the ruler from her desk. Placing his hand in her palm as was customary, the teacher drew back with the ruler, and as she brought it smashing downward, he withdrew his hand, leaving the teacher to swat her palm. She jumped, the spit wad fell off her nose, and she said a few bad words. Then he knew he was in trouble, and as he turned to run, she caught him by the back of his shirt and made him double up his fists and put them side by side on the edge of her desk. She held his wrist and brought the ruler smashing down on his knuckles once and twice, and the ruler broke in two as she hit the third time.

Soon afterward, it was time for recess, and all seemed okay. The teacher made up a game whereby everyone crawled between her legs, and she swatted them on their bottoms. Well, during these crawls, the swats became harder and harder, so he rose extra early, causing the teacher to flip over backward, and as she hit the ground, her head struck a rock so hard that she passed out. That same day, Grandpa was notified of what had happened, and that was why, after three days of school in the first grade, he was expelled from school and could not go back. That is why he didn't know how to read or write.

By now, we had long gone past the schoolhouse, up the big hill, and across the prairies to my godfather's farm, and we could see him in the yard awaiting our arrival.

Good Old Days

The car pulled to a squeaking halt, and all I had time for was to close my eyes as my godfather grabbed me and started to throw me into the air. The usual talk started, "He sure has grown, and he sure is gaining weight." To hear them carry on, by now I should be six feet tall, weighing two hundred pounds.

In the house, my godmother and Mom sat in the kitchen having coffee, as my godfather brought in a beer for himself and Dad into the living room. As he handed Dad his beer and stubbed his toe on the coffee table, he said a couple of words I already knew were no-nos. As I played on the floor with a few toys, I could hear Dad laughing. Cleo looked at him, saying, "Look, brother, I don't think it's very funny." Dad apologized and began to explain why he was laughing. Since it began to sound like a story, my ears perked up as I listened in.

"Don't you remember when we were in our teens, after we had finished herding the goats for three months, how we got home that Saturday morning, finding out that there was a dance at Bernal that night? We asked Dad if we could go to the dance, and he didn't give us permission to go because we had to go back out with the goats the following morning. Wanting to go so badly, we began to scheme as to how we could make it. So that night, you, Fred, and I got five-foot-long logs and placed them in our sleeping bags next to the house so that Dad would think we were asleep, then we saddled the horses and rode off to the dance. On returning that morning, we arrived back just minutes before Dad awoke, and as we were unsaddling the horses, we heard him scream bloody murder as he had just kicked the log in my sleeping bag."

About that time, my godfather interjected, "Yes," trying as hard as he could to stop laughing as he said, "Dad had broken his big toe, and remember how Fred immediately went running out, telling Dad that it was only you and I who had gone to the dance and that we were in the barn. At that time, I took advantage of the situation and took off running. From the distance, I saw Dad hobble his way to the barn and get a hold of you, taking the horsewhip off the wall, and start whipping you. Since you would not scream or yell, he ended up hitting you with the whip handle until he had cut your head open behind the right ear. About that time, Mom came out yelling at Dad, saying, 'Go ahead and kill him. He would be better off dead, for you treat the animals better.' But I must say, though you were dazed and hurting, you got up and ran the fastest, most crooked line up the hill I had ever seen."

Dad said, "Yeah, those were the good old days," as he finished his beer.

The conversation switched to the present, as I went back to playing with the toys. About that time, Ipa came in, hollering at me for some unknown reason, as Cleo said, "I see she is still on the bottle and wearing those combat boots," which only made Ipa mad as she spun about and left the room. As the day progressed, I must have fallen asleep, for when I awoke, we were turning into our driveway.

As Dad put the car in the garage, Mom was busy in the kitchen getting supper ready. We ate supper, and while Mom was doing the dishes, Dad took his coffee into the living room and helped me get ready for bed, for I was so tired.

Come to think of it, I never found out that Sunday how it came to be that I had been born in a boxcar, nor would I for years to come.

Naturally Talented

As each day came and passed, life was so exciting that I didn't even have time to notice that Mom had been getting everything ready for me to start school. I can surely bet that she was happy the day we walked into the school, and I met my first-grade teacher, Miss Burke. When Mom left me all alone with this stranger and walked out the door, she jumped in the air and clicked her heels.

All the time that I was there, I knew that something was different, but I just couldn't figure out what it was. Then suddenly, I realized that I was all alone in a room where everyone was speaking an entirely different language, which I soon found out was English, and that I was expected to know it yesterday.

School kept me so busy that I couldn't remember any school day with enough time left over to allow me to get into any good trouble. School had changed me so much that I was no longer that same boy, who was so full of life and could go from one incident into another, constantly in trouble. For now, all I had time to do was spend all my time learning this new language called English.

Time passed so fast that before I knew it, Christmas time was here, and the school was going to have a Christmas play. As the plans for the school play progressed, all the older kids made up the Christmas tree, and the younger ones were the maple dancers. As for me and Dolores, we had the main production number, doing a duet of a song called "Playmate," which we were to sing and act out. Dolores and I knew that we were tops, for we had been chosen because of our natural talents in acting and singing.

On the opening night, the auditorium was completely full, for all the parents had come. The curtain went up, and all was going so nicely as Dolores and I waited for our big break in showbiz. The end of the play came, and we walked to the center of the stage and began to do our number. I was so scared and began to stutter, then Dolores held my hand, and we sang our song. The applause came, and soon we were offstage and ready to embark on our careers in show business.

The rest of the year went by so fast, and oh, how happy I was that warm summer day, for summer vacation had started, and now I was determined to be myself again.

Speckled Forehead

Weeks had gone by, and how I managed to stay out of trouble, I just don't know. One Saturday morning, Mom took me with her to my Tia Amalia's house because she was going to help her prepare some pies, cakes, and all kinds of goodies, and I was in hopes that I might get to clean up the frosting bowl. We had been there about two hours when my aunt told Ambrose, who was about a year older than me, to get her some eggs from the chicken house. As Ambrose got ready to go, he told me to come along, and as we walked over to the chicken house, he picked up a large stick and gave it to me, saying, "There's a big mean rooster in there, and he doesn't like me to take the eggs out of the nests, so if you see him coming after me, hit him."

We got to the chicken house, and we both looked all around to see if we could see the rooster in the yard among the chickens, but he was nowhere in sight. As we opened the door to the chicken coop, the chickens began to make a lot of noise, so I got my stick ready, for the rooster was sure to come out now. Still, there was no rooster, so we proceeded into the coop and began to gather the eggs as Ambrose said, "I guess the rooster got out again." We started on one side and collected most of the eggs from the other side. As I put another egg into the basket Ambrose was holding, we both looked up for some unknown reason and behold, there was that mean rooster getting ready to jump down on us.

Sure enough, as the rooster began flapping his wings, Ambrose and I made a dash for the door, but it was too late. When the rooster landed on my head, I fought to get it off, and in the process, Ambrose and I ended up tripping each other. We both fell to the ground, him with the basket full of eggs crashing and breaking as they hit the ground and me still with the rooster holding on to my head. As I hit the ground, the rooster took a spill but was right back on top, pecking at my head and forehead. Then I noticed that the rooster was trying to get at my face, so I covered my face with my arms, from my eyes down. Ambrose got up, collected the four unbroken eggs, and ran yelling and screaming toward the house. Within a flash, both my aunt and Mom were in a dead run to my aid. As Mom picked me up, all she could see was that my face and head were covered with blood. For each time the rooster had pecked, he drew blood. Soon we were home, and Mom had cleaned me up, we were both happy that the rooster had not gotten my eyes, but even so, I ended up with iodine from my eyebrows up and a splitting headache, and it didn't take long to fall asleep.

Sunday came, and everything was the same as usual: Dad telling Mom to hurry, and my aunt waving her arms all around, except that after Mass, my aunt told us to come over for dinner. I still didn't feel too good and looked like a little Indian on the warpath with all the iodine on my forehead, but when my aunt said it was time to eat that mean old rooster that had gotten me, my appetite soared, and I sure felt great each time I took a bite of that mean old rooster.

Banana-Flavored Popsicle

As the days came and went, I stayed out of trouble well, until one very hot summer day. As I walked across to the playground, I saw that there must have been at least thirty kids out there, so I called my best friend over and asked him if he would like ice cream, and of course, the answer was yes. Soon all the kids were around me asking for ice cream. Well, now I had done it, for there was none at home, and they were beginning to think that I was lying. So as anyone in my position would do, I said, "Come with me, and you will get an ice cream, but only one." Off to the store we went like a company of soldiers. As we filed into the store, they all walked over to the cooler where the ice cream was, and I walked over to Mr. Wilbar and told him it was my birthday and Mom had said it was okay for me to buy my friends a popsicle or ice cream since it was so hot.

Not knowing that my birthday was still more than three months away, Mr. Wilbar went ahead and gave us each a popsicle or ice cream of whatever flavor we wanted. As everyone left the store, Mr. Wilbar called me aside and handed me a note to take to Mom. Of course, I was too smart for that, so I stuck the note in my pocket and planned to throw it away after I got outside. I took another bite of my banana-flavored popsicle and walked out the door, thanking Mr. Wilbar.

Before I realized it, it was Friday, which meant wash day, and I knew I had left the note in my pants. Being up extra early, I went to the washing machine and began to throw out all the clothes. Then realizing that I could really be in trouble, I began to put all the white clothes in one pile and all the others in another. I had no sooner finished than Mom came in, and as she saw all the clothes on the floor, I told her that it was washday and I was only trying to help. Well, Mom made breakfast, and after we were done, she told me to go out and play, which I did, but not for long. I was called in immediately when she found the note from Mr. Wilbar, and I was told I would have to explain it to Dad as soon as he got up.

Dad got up in a wonderful mood, and boy was I glad, for when I explained, all he said was I was getting too big for my britches, and from now on, I had to take a note to the store and that he was going to tell Mr. Wilbar not to give me anything unless I had a note. That sure put a stop to anything like that happening again since I could not write. And having come so close to getting tanned, I made up my mind to be an angel for the rest of the day.

Doña Feliz's Football

A few weeks had passed, and as usual for a Saturday, Ambrose and I would go out to the woodpile and collect wood chips for Doña Feliz. When Doña Feliz was a young girl, she had come to the States from Guadalupe, Mexico. She was a very nice old lady, who must have been at least one hundred years old because she was all wrinkled, but boy could she ever make the most delicious cactus candy. When Ambrose and I had finished collecting enough wood chips to last her until the next week, she would give us candy, but today she not only gave us the candy but also a real professional football which she had found. Ambrose and I stuffed the candy in our mouths and began to play with the football.

We were having so much fun and began to wonder how it would be possible to kick the ball way up in the sky. Then wow; the idea came to me that if we kicked the ball off the outhouse, which was about eight feet high, it would really go high. Soon we were climbing up on top of the outhouse. Once on top, the roof was about four feet wide and about five feet long. Up on the outhouse, it seemed like we were twenty feet off the ground.

Ambrose looked down and then said that he would hold the ball like in a football game and for me to back up, run, and kick the ball. He got as close as possible to the edge of the roof as I backed off in the opposite direction. I took off with a few quick steps and kicked the ball so hard that I went flying off the roof. The ball went higher and farther than ever before, as I came down, hitting the ground so hard. What was so funny was that I landed sitting down on my left foot, and my right foot was straight out in front of me.

Ambrose hollered from above, asking if I was okay. I assured him I was and how much fun it was, bragging about how far the ball had gone. I got up, betting Ambrose that he couldn't kick the ball farther. As I began to climb back up, I tried to convince him how much fun it was and that it was his turn to kick the football. Halfway up, I met Ambrose coming down, saying we should play in the field, but he never would admit that he was afraid of kicking the football off the outhouse. So we spent all day playing football, taking a break long enough to eat lunch and dinner.

Our Family Track Star

Sunday followed the same routine; soon we were off and heading toward my aunt's house. Here I was, all dressed up and so clean, and as we got about halfway past the big lot full of weeds so tall that I just could not resist the temptation to duck into them.

My aunt had her arms waving as usual, and Dad slowed his pace just to antagonize his sister. In a flash, I was gone, and almost as fast, Mom was telling Dad to make me get out before I got all dirty. Too late; for I was completely hidden by the tall weeds, and as I made my way toward my aunt's house, I saw a long black and brown round thing in front of me. My heart began to pound as I inched forward to take a closer look, and oh; what a relief because Mom had always said there were rattlesnakes in the field, and this was only a piece of hose.

I began to walk on by, but I just had to pick it up. Mom and Dad were just about five feet from my aunt and uncle as I came running out of the field with the hose in one hand, shaking it from side to side, and began yelling, "Look, Mom. I found a rattlesnake."

My aunt took off running, hollering holy something, as her feet kicked up the dust, and Mom screamed and called Dad's name and took off running after my aunt—boy could she run fast. Dad grabbed me by the arm and told me it was not funny, even though Uncle Flavio was already laughing, and as he took the hose out of my hand, he just could not hold it back anymore, and he began to laugh. My uncle was laughing so loud as he made comments about Mom, the track star, for not only had she caught up with my aunt but had left her in the dust. As we continued on our way to church, Dad told my uncle that they better control their laughter about the track stars, or they were going to be in trouble.

Soon we had caught up with the track stars and continued our way to church, and as we neared the garage, I noticed that the train engine and a lot of boxcars were lying on their side as I took off in a dead run.

Looking back, I could see Dad gaining on me, and as I reached the intersection, his arm reached forward, landing on my right shoulder, which stopped me in my tracks with one foot still in midair. As we stood there, I noticed that a boxcar had rolled down off the tracks, across the street, and was resting on its side right up against the church door.

Up the street, for as far as you could see, there were boxcars in the road, on the lawns, and a few even on some porches. Streetlights had been broken and only pieces remained, as they were made of cement.

Time for Mass came and passed when I began to hear popping sounds, and as I looked at where they were coming from, I noticed men with rifles. As we continued to watch, the two giant cranes worked hard to pick up the big locomotive and set it back on the tracks. I finally convinced Dad to go across the road because I wanted to find out what the men with rifles were doing. So across the road, we went, and up to the tracks where I saw one of the men shoot a steer with his rifle.

Dad explained to me that the animal could not be saved and that it was suffering very much, and that the men shot it so it would not suffer anymore. We then went home and ate breakfast, and I actually asked permission to spend the rest of the day watching the cranes putting all the boxcars back on the track or on flatbeds so they could be taken away.

The Devil Gets the Best of Me

It was just impossible to believe that these days had the same number of hours, for there I was going back to school, and it seemed that during summer vacation each day was so short, and yet at school each day was always so long. The first month at school went by fast, and I could hardly wait for payday to come because my birthday was just a few days away.

I constantly kept trying to find out what I was going to get for my birthday, and it seemed like the more I tried to find out, the more persistent Mom was that I was not going to get anything. Payday came, and off to the big city of Florence we went, Dad driving, and my uncle Flavio in front, with Mom, my aunt Amalia, and myself in the back. As we approached the outskirts of Florence, I noticed that Mom's purse was open, and there in the center stood a five-dollar bill, just staring at me and daring me to take it. I knew it was wrong, and I kept telling myself I was not going to do it. Unknown to me, my right hand inched over very slowly and so cautiously, making sure that Mom would not notice, and pulled out the five dollars and put it in my pocket. Needless to say, I was so surprised and could not believe that my hand had done it, and was sure the devil had made it do it.

But yet as we came to a stop in front of the five-and-ten-cent store, I could not bring myself to tell Mom, "Here's the five dollars the devil took out of your purse," because I knew she would not believe me. As we got out of the car, I asked if I could stay in front of the five-and-ten-cent store and look at all the toys in the window, and was so surprised when I was given permission. They all walked across the street, and as Mom and my aunt went to Senatore's, my uncle and Dad went to the Oasis to have a few beers while the women shopped.

As I stood there looking at all the toys, I could hear this big, bright red tractor with all the attachments for everything, say to me, "We could sure have a lot of fun. Come in and buy me, please." I kept trying to fight off the temptation by reminding myself of how much trouble I was already in, but you know what, that devil is something else because he didn't stop bothering me until I was back in the car, trying to figure out how I was going to hide the great big tractor and the attachments. I managed to lift the seat and placed everything under the seat and had finished placing the seat back and sat down as everyone returned. With packages all over the back seat, we pulled out and headed out of town and on our way back to Portland.

Having gone about seven miles out of town, Dad turned off the main road, and as we headed for a ranch, he turned and said, "Now we are going to get your birthday present." We came to a stop as we neared the well in front of the house. Dad and I got out of the car and walked over to the well. Then he hollered down to someone that he was here to pick it up. Within a few minutes, the rancher came out holding the cutest, fattest, and fluffiest brown, black, and white puppy I had ever seen. My eyes were so big with surprise, and my heart pounded so fast as Dad handed me the puppy and asked what I was going to name it. As I answered I was going to call him Jackie, I began to cry. Dad put his arms around me and said, "We wouldn't forget your birthday because we love you very much," and then I really started crying because I felt so bad because of what I had done. Before we got back into the car, I was crying so much that it was almost impossible to tell Dad what I had done, and between sobs, I told him how sorry I was and that I would never do it again and that I did not deserve to have the puppy.

Dad bent down, and as he wiped the tears from my eyes, he said, "Since you told me, and you won't do it again"—he put his arms around me with the puppy between us—"the puppy is still yours, so stop crying."

We got back in the car and left the ranch, heading for home with me holding Jackie in my lap, and once back on the main road, Dad told Mom what had happened to the five dollars.

Through the Briar and the Bramble

Back to those extra-long days I went, for I was back in school and now in the second grade, and my teacher was Ms. Lameire, who appeared to be nicer than Ms. Burke. Oh, what a year this was going to be, for now I could understand English, and I would have more free time to be myself.

It must have been the fourth or fifth week after school had started that, for some reason on that Saturday, I could not think of anything to do. So I went to my aunt's to see if Ambrose could play, and she told me that he and Connie were up on the hill herding the goats.

That really excited me because Dad had herded goats when he was my age, and now I could find out how it was done. Up the hill I went, stopping to catch my breath a few times. When I finally got up to the top of the hill, I noticed a big wooden barrel just sitting there, empty and ready to roll down the hill. But just then, I saw Ambrose and Connie in a ditch, waving their arms, about a block away, so off I went running to where they were.

After getting about halfway there, I saw why they were in the ditch and came to such a fast stop that I slid and fell. I just couldn't get up fast enough as I saw the billy goat jump over Ambrose, Connie, and the ditch, and head straight for me at full speed ahead.

With that billy goat coming at me faster than a speeding bullet, I didn't have to tell my feet to run because they were already in motion, and going so fast that I thought they would leave me behind. As I ran to get off the hill, I could see the barrel, and right away, my mind flashed back to the rodeo I had seen last summer how the clowns got into the barrel and the big bulls would leave them alone. But would it work on this billy goat?

Into the barrel I went and had no sooner crouched down as the billy goat hit the barrel with a crash so loud, I thought it would fall apart. The barrel fell over and went rolling down the hill with me inside of it. Faster and faster the barrel went as I kept trying to crawl out without success, only to continue to roll inside the barrel as we went faster and faster, flying into the air each time we hit a bump or rock. It seemed like I had been in that barrel for hours when finally, it began to slow down and finally came to a stop.

I grabbed my head with both hands, hoping it would stop my head from spinning so fast. I tried to crawl out but only fell down, for I was so dizzy that I just lay there and let the tears come out while the whole world just went round and round, and all I wanted to do was to go home to Mom.

My head and the whole world finally stopped spinning; I wiped the tears from my eyes as I noticed I was right in the middle of all the thorn bushes in the ravine. As I got ready to get out, I saw this black umbrella lying a few feet from me. Then the idea came to me to open the umbrella partway and use it as a shield, so I wouldn't get too many thorns in me. Through the bushes, I went without too much trouble as I saw Ambrose coming about halfway down the hill, asking what I had found.

Each time before, when I found something, Ambrose had always taken it away from me, and this time I was determined that he would not. I went through the bushes so fast that I didn't notice that two panels had been ripped off, and as I headed for home with my umbrella, Ambrose was close behind.

In the yard now, and I felt safe, so I opened the umbrella and began walking to the house as Ambrose caught up, saying, "Oh, I thought it was good, but it's not. Give it to me, and I'll fix it, and we both can play with it."

"No," I said as he then asked to hold it for a while. Then the fight started as he reached for it because I was not going to give in. Both of us going round and round, him holding one end and me the other, and somewhere in the process, my thumb got in his mouth and his teeth came clamping down around my thumb like a bear trap. Then I cried out in pain as Mom came out of the house, but it was too late, for Ambrose was running off with my umbrella. Into the house, I went and cried myself to sleep.

The next morning before Mass, Ambrose came over with the umbrella and said I could have it, but I told him to keep it because after the fight the day before, two more panels had been ripped off, and it looked so funny with only two panels now.

Soon we were all on our way to church, and as we walked, Dad began talking about his son Tony, which he explained was due to come home from the war because he had been wounded.

Wrong Kind of Rabbit

I didn't think much about Tony because school occupied most of my time, and it sure didn't seem like time had gone by so fast. But here it was October, and almost time for my birthday again, and it was Friday already. I always liked Fridays because then I had the weekends to cram full of fun before school on Monday.

As Ambrose and I got to my house after school, Mom was in the yard, and as she handed me a note, she told me to go to the store for a few things and asked Ambrose to help me. Off we headed for the store with Jackie, my dog, going in front of us, for he went with me everywhere, even to school. He was the only dog that could go inside, mainly because they couldn't keep him out, and he was so attentive that the teacher told Mom that she was thinking of giving him a report card.

We had finished crossing the playground and were about half a block from the store when Jackie began growling at a dog that had foam coming out of its mouth. As we got closer, Jackie backed up and started pushing us to the side, making us stay as far away as possible from the other dog. When we got to the parking lot, there was a lady putting groceries in her car.

We had no sooner got inside the store when she came in and told Mr. Wilbar that there was a rabid dog in the lot. We began getting everything Mom wanted as Mr. Wilbar went out the door with his rifle. As we put everything on the counter, we heard the shot, and soon Mr. Wilbar came in and marked everything down. After leaving the store, we noticed the dog had been shot in the head, and when we tried to get close, Jackie pushed us away. Soon we were at my house, and Ambrose was on his way home.

Cold Potbelly Stove Puts Out Smoke

Saturday morning, and I had no sooner finished eating breakfast than my aunt and uncle arrived, and Ambrose was with them. It seemed so strange at first, but then I realized that it was payday because that was the normal procedure since last year. Ambrose and I could stay together as our two sisters tried to watch us. Soon our parents were on their way, and outside we went to find something to do for a couple of hours.

Ipa came out of the house and hollered that it was ten till eight, so in the house we ran, for at eight o'clock, all the good programs on the radio started, such as *Sparkie*, *Theater 25*, *The Lone Ranger*, and *Howdy Doody*. The radio was on, and the announcer came on as Ipa said she was going over to see Charlotte, which was fine with us because then it would be quiet.

The *Lone Ranger* program had just started when I noticed the carton of cigarettes on the radio. I looked at Ambrose and reached for a pack of cigarettes and opened it. It wasn't long at all before we forgot about the stories and began smoking one cigarette after another. We each tried to outdo the other by seeing who could blow rings or make the smoke come out of our noses and ears. We were having so much fun that soon the second pack was gone, and now we were really trying the hard stuff, like making the smoke go up our nose, or even worse yet, inhaling the smoke. Inhaling was so hard because each time we would cough so hard our eyes almost came out of our heads and would be so full of tears that we finally gave up trying to inhale. We had just opened the fourth pack during our contest to see who could have the longest ash before it fell off.

The program *Howdy Doody* came on the air, and we knew the folks would be home before too long. We put what was left of the fourth pack of cigarettes back in the carton when we noticed that the house was full of smoke. I had opened the back door, and as I returned to the room, Ambrose opened the front door, and there stood our dads. As they looked in, they asked why the house was so full of smoke.

"Oh, Dad, this potbelly stove just kept letting out smoke, and that is why the room is so full of smoke, isn't that right, Ambrose?"

"Oh yes, that's what happened," Ambrose said.

Dad reached over to the stove, placing his hand on it. He looked at my uncle and said, "For the stove being cold, it sure put out a lot of smoke." As they sat on the sofa, they told us to sit down between them, and Dad reached into the bag and brought out a box of cigars. As he handed one to my uncle and got one for himself, he placed the box in front of Ambrose and me and told us to go ahead and get one since we thought we were old enough to smoke.

Oh no, I wasn't about to get one because the smell alone got me sick, but before we had a chance to say anything, each of our dads reached forward, and we found ourselves with a cigar in our mouths, and now they had the match to the end of them as they told us to suck in. How we managed to get them lit with all the gagging and coughing was something else.

Then the bad news came: "Since you like to smoke, we're going to sit here and watch you smoke each one, or else you get the belt." We smoked, and we smoked until we had gotten about halfway finished with the box, but we were so sick we could not even look at another one, our faces were turning green, and our eyes were all red and on fire.

Then Dad grabbed me and gave me a spanking and warned me that he better not catch me smoking again. After that ordeal, I knew I would never smoke again because I was so sick and sore that all I wanted was to go to bed, but Dad wouldn't let me because he said I wasn't sick and to go outside and play. Who could play? My stomach wanted to come out of my body, my bottom ached with each step, my mouth tasted like I had eaten rotten eggs, and my eyes felt like they were going to pop out. Not even a dead person could feel this bad, but I was supposed to play.

That night I went to sleep extra early, and if I did not wake up, it was okay with me. Sunday morning came, and I felt a whole lot better, but I guess not good enough to get into any trouble.

Poker Poker

Who's Got the Poker

Another week of school went by, and it must have been about seven-thirty in the morning that Saturday when a big green Buick stopped in front of our house. Dad was outside, and as he called for Mom, these two big, tall guys got out of the car in uniforms with their buttons and medals shining. Then I remembered that one of these two guys must be my brother Tony. Dad hugged one of them as Mom came out of the front door, and as Dad shook hands with the other one, I then knew which one was my brother.

It must have been about nine o'clock when I realized I still had not had breakfast, and everyone was still out on the porch talking. I asked a couple of times as to when we were going to eat, but no one heard me. So I went into the kitchen and began to get my own breakfast. I put the skillet over the fire and then climbed up on a chair so I could put the eggs into the skillet. As I stood there watching the grease get hot and begin to smoke, I realized that something was wrong because my eggs were not getting done. Mom, having smelled the grease burning, came rushing in from outside, and everyone followed behind her. Mom got her potholder and removed the skillet from the wood and coal stove and then began to laugh, and soon everyone was laughing when they saw that I had put a dozen eggs in the skillet without breaking the shell. Mom then fixed breakfast, and as soon as I had finished, I went out to play as the others sat at the table drinking coffee.

It wasn't too long, and I was back in the house next to my big brother, and as I saw the situation then, it was really going to be nice to have a big brother because as soon as I could get him aside, I was going to tell him about my big sister, and that way he could protect me from her. But the day went by so fast that I never got to talk to him.

Sunday morning, and I was up early as usual, and Mom was already in the kitchen fixing breakfast when I looked up at the clock and realized that it was almost time for church. I went into the living room and asked Dad if we were going to church, and to my surprise, he said no.

Back into the kitchen, I went and sat there watching Mom make pancakes and syrup, and that syrup sure did smell good. A large pile of pancakes was on a plate on top of the stove. I asked if I could eat and was told that I would have to wait until my brother and his friend got up. I very politely said okay and went into the living room.

As I waited with my mouth watering and my stomach aching from being so empty, I began thinking that my brother would never get up unless someone woke him up. When Dad walked into the kitchen to have a cup of coffee, I sneaked into the bedroom where my brother and his friend were sleeping on one big bed. I walked over to the bed and began to shake my brother's arm when all at once his arm flung back at me as all he did was mumble and moan. Now I really began to wonder if they would ever get up, and I wasn't about to try and shake him again because this time, his arm might hit me.

The house smelled so good with that freshly made hot maple syrup, and I could just see it running down over my buttered pancakes, but I had to wait, so to occupy my time, I began to poke the hot ashes in the potbelly stove in the living room with the poker and was having fun when Dad called me from the kitchen. I put the red-hot poker in the coal bucket and went to see what he wanted, hoping that I was finally going to be able to eat. Dad asked if my brother was up and if not for me to wake him up. I was really glad because now it was okay to get them up. As I went through the living room, I saw that the poker was still hot because the end of it was still red. As I walked into the bedroom, I grabbed the poker and very quietly walked to the foot of the bed. Carefully I lifted the blankets off their feet so I would not wake them. There before me stood four big feet sticking straight up in the air. I lifted the poker and got it in position to make sure that the red-hot tip would not touch their feet, and in a flash, I brought the poker forward, touching all four feet at once.

Two yells came out in stereo, and never before had two guys get out of bed so fast in their lives, landing on the floor doing an Indian war dance as they grabbed for each foot. I took the opportunity at that time to get out of the room very quickly and into the kitchen to tell Dad that they were up, but of course not telling him how I had gotten them up. They both came into the kitchen, and they each stared at me, and I was surprised that they did not tell Dad about me. Shortly after breakfast, my brother's friend decided he had to go, as he explained to my brother he just could not think of spending another morning here.

Halloween and the Snowstorm

My birthday came and passed without much to do, for Mom was about to have a baby. That night, it began to snow lightly, and winter was coming early because we never had snowfall until after Halloween.

It was still snowing the next morning, and after breakfast, I put on my jacket and went out with Tony to bring in some wood and coal for the stoves. When we finished, he even came out, and we had a snowball fight.

It continued to snow all day and night, and by the next morning, it was three feet deep most everywhere and deeper in other areas where the wind had piled it up, but now the snow was starting to subside.

I found out later that early that morning before I awoke, Dad had walked to Dr. Davis's to have him call for an ambulance to come from Florence and take my mother to the hospital.

After returning from Dr. Davis's, Dad had gone to my uncle Flavio's and other friends and cousins to get help in clearing a path from the cement road to the house so the ambulance could come and get Mom.

That was what woke me up when I heard the siren of the ambulance as it came to get Mom. They took care of Mom and put blankets on her so she would not get cold, and they put her inside the ambulance, and Dad also got inside. They closed the doors and took off with the siren going and the lights flashing. As they made their way to the cement road, you could just see the top of the ambulance with its light going round and round.

I then asked Tony how Dad was going to come home since he did not take the car. He told me that Uncle Flavio would be going to pick him up the following day.

The skies cleared, and the sun was shining by eleven o'clock, and the snow was starting to melt.

The next morning, the sun was shining through the icicles that were all around the house and casting different colors on the walls when Tony and I went out to get more wood, collect the eggs, and feed the chickens and the rabbits.

I don't remember if it was the day before or the day of Halloween that Mom finally came back home from the hospital with my baby brother. But I do remember that evening after supper while we ate our pumpkin pie, Tony began to tell us scary stories about witches and ghosts. It began to get dark, and I was sent out to get more wood, and as I walked out the door, Tony said, "Look out for the witches and ghosts because tonight is Halloween, and they are all out there." I ran to the woodpile, bringing in four loads in record time, and when I got the fifth load in my arm, I looked up, and there at Doña Feliz's shed stood a shadow.

"Forget this wood." I threw the wood up in the air as I began to run to the house. At the same time, the shadow ran in front of her house and over to the edge of the garage.

I ran inside and closed the door, and Tony asked me what was wrong. I didn't answer for a while because I was scared stiff. Finally, I told him about the shadow I had seen. He told me I was just seeing things. I looked out the kitchen window, and the shadow was still there. I told Tony to come and see for himself that the shadow was still there.

Tony looked out for a while and then decided to go and check it out. My big brother was going to go check it out but wanted me to go with him so that I could see there was nothing to be afraid of. Out the door, I went with him, not that I wanted to, but he had a hold of my left arm with his right hand. We had only gone about ten feet from the kitchen door when the shadow took off running as before, but as fast as it got to the garage before your eyes could look back to the shed, there it was again. Tony hesitated and yelled out at whatever it was, but there was no response. So we continued toward it, as it continued to make its arc; as we got ten feet closer.

We finally got to about where it made its arc, and as it started again, Tony pushed me in front of it while still holding onto my arm. I saw the shadow coming, and zoom—it went through me, and the next thing I remember is being inside the kitchen with the door locked and Tony staring back at me, all pale and his eyes bulging out.

The next day we checked for tracks and never found any, and we never found out what it was.

Sheets and Sheets of Chocolate

Spring arrived, and with it came Easter vacation, which turned out to be an Easter vacation I will never forget. The school had let out on Thursday, so on Friday morning, our entire family went across the street by the playground to help my cousins, the Castellanos, move in. They had a boy, and it didn't take long for us to get to know each other. Soon we were out at the playground, for in their house, we only got in the way.

After introducing George to all the kids there at the playground and having played so many different games, we became thirsty, and instead of going to his house, we went across to my house so that we could get a drink of water. Walking into the house through the front door and noticing that no one was there, not even my sister, we went into the kitchen and got our drink of water. We had just walked out of the kitchen when I remembered that there was a big box of chocolates in the china cabinet. I asked George if he liked chocolate candy, and zoom, we were in the room where the china cabinet was and closed the door behind us so no one would know we were there. I climbed up on the cabinet and opened the big box of chocolates.

At first, I took out two individual sheets of candy which contained about twenty-four individual pieces of candy. Handing one to George, he sat down in a chair as I sat on the edge of the cabinet, and we began eating the biggest Hershey bars we had ever seen. For two kids who liked chocolate so much, it didn't take long for us to finish the first sheet.

Each individual piece of chocolate had the letters "Ex-Lax," and as far as we knew, it was a new brand of Hershey bars because they were not as sweet as usual, but they were still good enough for us to continue eating them.

We had eaten all the chocolate in the box and were about halfway finished with the last two sheets of chocolate when our mothers came in catching us in the act and to our surprise did not yell at us. George's mom went to get Doctor Davis, and now we were both scared, for Mom was acting as if we had eaten poison instead of chocolate.

Doctor Davis arrived, and with him came his little black bag full of needles, pills, and little wooden sticks that made you want to throw up. He opened the little black bag as he found out what we had eaten, and out came a bottle of little white pills. He handed us each a pill as our mothers gave us a glass of water. George took his pill as I continued to protest that I was not sick and felt okay. Within a few minutes, as I turned to ask George if the pill tasted good, I saw his eyes widen, as his cheeks bulged out with his hands going up to his mouth, and I knew what was coming up next. All I could think of was what an awful waste of good chocolate.

I put the pill under my tongue and drank the water, pretending to have taken the pill. Doctor Davis left, assuring our mothers that the pill would work. It seemed like so much time had passed, for now, the pill was beginning to dissolve in my mouth. It had such an awful taste that I began to gag as I made a dash for the back door. Out the back door, I went and didn't get more than three or four steps as everything started coming up but just couldn't make it all the way. Hours must have gone by before I was able to stop gagging. As the days passed, I sure wished that I had swallowed the pill because, for at least three days after that, I became the best of buddies with the old outhouse.

Hippety-Hoppity All the Way Home

With Easter vacation over and back at school, we found out that in two weeks, we would no longer go to school in Portland, everyone would be going to school in Florence, and my class was going to McCandles Grade School. It seemed to take forever, but the day finally came, and everyone was so happy because now we would be able to ride a great big yellow bus all the way to and from Florence for the rest of the school year. Even though I had to get up earlier now that we took the bus to school, I didn't mind because it was so much fun, and time went by so fast that it was hard to believe that a week could go by so fast.

That Saturday, Ipa and I were arguing as we always did when we were in the house at the same time, when all at once, she grabbed me and threw me so hard into a big easy chair with high arms that it knocked the breath out of me. Then to make matters worse, she sat on me, and with her weight on top of me, I sank in so far into the chair that I could not be seen, and only my muffled cries for help could be heard as Mom came in to see what was going on. She asked Ipa where I was, and Ipa said she didn't know and that she was being good and was only sitting in the chair. About that time, I managed to work one of my arms out from behind her. Mom pulled Ipa off me, and I was so happy because now I could breathe again. But I was so boiling mad that I hauled off and with my fist hit Ipa smack dead in the right eye so hard that before she could stop crying, she had the most beautiful black eye. But I must admit that when Dad got home from work, she told Dad that she had run into the doorknob, or else

I could have been black and blue in more places than one because I was a boy, and boys never hit girls no matter what.

Sunday came, and things were normal as usual until about ten o'clock when Tony came and brought a girl with him in his new car and told us she was going to be his wife and that her name was Mary Lou. As they sat down to have coffee, I went out to play in the big lot on the other side of Ambrose's house, where the day before I had watched some men making a lot of holes big enough for railroad ties, which were to be used as posts for a fence. Tony's new car went by and, seeing four people in it, I wished I had been home because then I could have gotten a ride in his new car. But then it didn't bother me because, with everyone gone, I could now go home and get some candy out of the china cabinet.

I got home and went to the back door in case Ipa was in the front part of the house, and that way she would not see me. As I opened the back door, I saw Mary Lou at the sink, and as I started to walk in with my muddy shoes, she hollered at me to stay out. My plans having been ruined, I got mad as I told her I wanted a drink of water and that I didn't have to do anything she told me because she wasn't my mother. With that said, muddy shoes and all, I walked in and got my drink of water. She very bluntly told me to hurry up and get out so she could re-mop the floor.

About that time, Dad looked into the kitchen from the living room and saw what was happening. I dropped the glass into the sink and heard the glass shatter as I reached the back door. Through the back door, I went and started running around the front of the house, only to see Dad come out the front door instead of the kitchen door.

Running up the road toward my aunt's house I went, looking back only after I had passed the empty field between our houses. I could see Dad getting closer as he worked to get his new belt off. Uncle Flavio was working in the front yard as Dad called out to him to catch me. Now I really was afraid because I could just see myself cut to ribbons with that new belt, for it was four inches wide, and all over it, from the buckle to the end of it, it had small rhinestones and silver and gold buttons which stuck out about a quarter of an inch.

Uncle Flavio came toward me a few steps, stopped, and took his position, remaining there waiting to catch me. Now how was I ever going to get out of this? With a quick fake to the left and recovery to the right at full speed, his left hand just missed me as I headed for the field by his house.

"Go, Abel, go," I could hear my uncle say as Dad whisked by him and was right behind me as I ran through the weeds, jumping each hole that had been made for the railroad ties. After passing the fourth hole, I heard a big thud as I heard Dad cry out, "Aha!" followed by a few moans. I stopped immediately as I knew for sure that he had really been hurt badly. I began to inch my way back as I remembered he still had the belt. Closer and closer I went, not more than an inch at a time, to see if Dad was okay, and then as I was just out of his arm's reach, I saw that he was still there with his left foot up to his chest and his right foot still in the hole.

Dad looked at me with such an expression on his face and said, "Help me, son. I think I broke my leg." I just couldn't resist, and as I reached for him, he grabbed me good and tight as he said, "Now I'll show you how bad my leg really is."

Now Dad had me on his right side, holding my left arm with his left hand, and though I could not see the belt, I just knew that Dad's right hand was free and holding that belt behind me. Suddenly, with a great big bang, I came jumping out of the weeds, for the belt had struck its first of many times. As I walked and Dad limped down the road on our way home, and about each time I took three steps to his two, the belt would hit its mark as I would jump into the air, not so much from the force but mostly from the pain. I tried everything I could so it wouldn't hurt so much, from jumping before the belt hit, only to be hit on the back of the legs, and when I didn't jump, I got it on the back. Oh, I was so sore and became so happy when we finally reached home, for then the belt went back around Dad's waist.

For the next month and a half or so, all I had to do was remember all the little black and blue places on my entire backside, and I had no problem staying out of trouble, especially when Dad would see me start doing something wrong. All he had to say was, "Do you want the belt?"

GEORGE SOLANO

I would stop dead in my tracks and not move, although that little devil in my mind kept saying, "Tell him yes, then you can take the belt and burn it," but I knew better than to do something like that.

Mom's Heart Gets Broken

Days upon days, Mom and Dad had been cleaning all the furniture and packing everything in boxes. Even the china cabinet, where the candy was always kept, was completely taken apart and repainted, and just before payday, Dad had almost gotten it all back together. Payday came, and Mom and Dad went to Florence as usual, and this time it took them all day, which was very unusual. When they returned, I asked why it had taken so long, and that was when I found out that in three weeks, we would be moving to Florence. Boy, I just couldn't wait to make the move because we would be going from this small town with a population of 183 to the great big city of Florence, which had a population of 2,347. As the groceries and everything else were being put away, I went outside to the playground and let everyone know that we were going to move to Florence.

Sunday came, and with all the normal things out of the way, I was out at the playground when I saw a car drive up to the house. The car, looking familiar, I paid more attention, and when I noticed that it was Fidel and his wife, I took off for home. They only came over once in a while because they lived in Pueblo, and that was thirty-two miles away, but when they did come to visit, I always wanted to be at home because he would always give me some money, and I was always in hopes that she would bring my baby shoes so I could see how small my feet used to be, and to this day, as far as I know, she still has my baby shoes.

That afternoon, it must have been about two or three o'clock because it had just been long enough after lunch that I was hungry again. Since we were all in the living room, I walked out the front door, saying I was going to go play with Ambrose. Out the door and through the gate, I went as I turned left and headed for Ambrose's house.

I had gotten just past our yard when I decided to go through the weeds in the empty lot and back into the house through the kitchen door. I reached the back door, and as the door was open, I could see that no one was in the kitchen, so I opened the screen door very slowly so the spring would not make any noise, just wide enough for me to get in. I turned and let it close very quietly. With four very soft steps, I reached the room where the china cabinet was and closed the door so quietly that the click of the door knob was not heard.

I crawled up on the cabinet and began to reach for the door where the candy was, for now I was going to satisfy my hunger. The door was stuck, as it often became, so I began to pull harder on it. Still not being able to open the door, I yanked on it with all my might, only to see the entire top half of the cabinet start coming at me. I slid off the cabinet and crawled under the big round table just in time, as the top half of the cabinet came crashing down on the table.

The glass in the doors shattered into a million pieces as Mom's brand-new set of china, which she had bought just the day before, came crashing all over the table and floor. Hundreds and thousands of pieces of glass and china were all that remained of Mom's china, as everyone in the house came rushing into the room.

Mom cried as she saw her beautiful china in pieces all over the floor, and as she reached down to pick up the small saucer and coffee cup that remained unshattered, she told Dad that it never would have happened had he finished putting the cabinet back together with the screws that held on the top half. As Mom started to get up with a tear running down her cheek, she noticed that I was under the table. She immediately told Dad that I was just lying there under all the rubble. Everything was up and out of the way in no time at all. Dad reached down under the table and picked me up, looking to see if I had been cut by some of the glass or hurt, but all that was wrong with me was that I was as white as a sheet of paper, for I had been so scared. Though Mom's heart had been broken, I still wondered why I didn't get the belt; perhaps because they were so glad I had not been injured because having company over had never stopped them before.

Florence, Here We Come

Summer was gone, and it was time to go to school again. I never could get used to having so little time out of school, and school always seemed to last for more than a year, in fact, almost two. Back in school, I could not really pay attention because I was so excited about moving that each day just seemed to last forever. But to my disappointment, little did I realize that while I spent those first two weeks in school, Dad had been busy moving almost everything, and on Friday of the second week, I found out that everything had been moved, and I hadn't had the chance to help. Off to school, I went on that last Friday, and it seemed like it would never end, but finally, the last school bell rang, and out I went running, passing up Ipa on the way to the big yellow bus. The ride back to Portland seemed to last forever, especially with each stop the bus made. Dad had told us that morning that he would pick us up behind the cement plant, at the bus stop near the old schoolhouse. When the bus finally turned right at the cement plant, I could see Dad standing next to Mom in front of the car with his arms folded, patiently waiting for us. The bus finally got to the bus stop, and when the doors opened, they almost slapped my face because I was ready to go. Off the bus, I flew and ran to Dad, and as I got into the car, I could see slowpoke Ipa just getting off the bus. Finally, Ipa made it to the car, and everyone was ready to go.

Up the dirt road, we went over the railroad tracks by the cement plant and turned left on the main highway. We went in front of the cement plant, passed Mr. Wilbar's store, then the church, and rounded the corner at the end of town, headed on our way to Florence.

As we entered the town of Florence, we passed the feed store on the right side, across a garage, a Ford garage on the right, across the magnet bar, and a mineralogy store. Across each other at the intersection was the First National Bank and the *Citizen Newspaper*, then with Jim the Tailor on the right and senators on the left, Safeway was on the right, across the Oasis, and across the malt shop was the hardware store. There was another intersection, and on the left were the Florence Hotel and the Rialto Theater, and across it was Vandettie's, and on the left was the Green Parrot. There was another intersection, and still on the left side was the Phillips gas station, and on the right was the police and fire station.

We continued going straight, then went over the tracks and turned right after three blocks to First Street. Dad brought the car to a halt in front of the third house at the end of the street.

"Wow." I guess we were rich now because we were going to live in a two-story mansion. It had four huge bedrooms and an indoor bathroom upstairs, and downstairs was an enormous kitchen, living and dining room, plus two huge rooms that became a porch.

Next to the house were five cherry trees, each of a different type, with a fountain in the center of them. Behind the cherry trees were the grapevines and the snowball tree, which made the best archery bows in town. Behind the house and to the left was a garage, which had been made into a two-room house for Doña Feliz at the end of the yard, and next to her house was the coal shed. In front of the coal shed was a big peach tree. Next to the coal shed was the gate, and next to it was an old outhouse with the ash pit next to it, followed by the woodshed and the garage. Behind all this was a narrow alley and the railroad tracks.

For the rest of that school year, Ipa and I would catch the school bus in front of the house and go to McCandless on the other side of town. The following year, I went to Emerson, and Ipa went to junior high.

For the next few years, nothing much happened that really meant much, just a few things like holding my own with the neighborhood bullies, the Riveras, by learning quickly that a big stick was a good equalizer. The years passed as I explored the hills between

Florence and Rockville, checking out all the caves and old mine shafts, and now that I was ten, I was too smart to get into trouble. Besides, I was always away from the house, so I could do almost anything and not get caught.

Grape Juice vs. Wine

Ch vs. *Sh*

Each winter, I never got into trouble because, after school, all I ever did was chop wood and take in coal for the stove and furnace, and then sit in front of the TV all night. During summer vacation that year, I made my decision to pursue the road to sainthood because I was going to be an altar boy. Each Saturday morning, we would gather at the father's house and practice our lines, which were in Latin. The father would pronounce them, and we would repeat them until we had them memorized, even though we never knew what their meaning was.

One Saturday morning, as my turn came to read a sentence in Latin, which was "que fay chit chair loom et ter nam," I remember seeing stars and cuckoo birds just rolling around in my head because the priest had slapped me so hard. That was when I learned to pronounce *ch* instead of *sh*, and thereafter, I always pronounced that sentence correctly.

Having mastered the language in a few weeks, I became an altar boy, and in the six months following, I had served high, low, and medium masses, even weddings and funerals, and always wondered each time I poured the wine if it really was wine. Month after month, I would pour the leftover wine down the drain. Then early one Sunday morning, I had to serve mass all by myself since the other altar boy did not show up, and that day, the priest used more water than wine.

Mass was over, and the priest quickly got out of his vestments and put them away as I went back to the altar to move the epistle back to the left side. Then as I went back to the sacristy and the priest had already gone, I took the candle snuffer and went back to the altar. As I finished snuffing out the candles, the last two people walked out the door. Back in the sacristy all by myself, I began putting away all the other items. Now with everything in its place, I walked over to the sink to pour out and clean the water and wine pitchers.

The birds were singing, the flowers were in bloom, the sun was up, and the promise was there for a warm and beautiful day as I looked out the window over the sink. I finished drying the water pitcher and tray, and as I grabbed the wine pitcher, I wondered, as always, if it was really wine or just grape juice, as I had often heard. I lifted the wine pitcher high in the air in front of the window with the sun shining through it, as I began to pour it out of the pitcher, with it flowing down in a steady stream into my open mouth. My taste buds went crazy and became very warm as the sweet flavor of the wine spread throughout and warmed each part of me on its way to my stomach. Everything having been cleaned and having put away my tunic and cassock, I walked home singing all the way, "Oh, what a wonderful day."

Mason Jar

Spring came early the following year, and the days seemed so warm simply because winter had been so cold. School was not out yet, and I was still learning Latin each Saturday at three o'clock at the father's house, which was next to the church. So each Saturday, to occupy my time after having chopped wood and cleaning the yard, I would walk out the back gate between the coal shed and the old outhouse, turning left in the alley, walking about half a block to the road, where upon crossing the road, I would walk, balancing myself on one of the train tracks for about two blocks, going over the creek.

Once I got to the hole in the fence by the oil well on the left side of the train tracks, I would go down to the creek and begin crisscrossing the creek as I walked down the creek under the road leading to the grade school. Not far from the bridge, the creek straightened out, and from there, I could see Peggy waiting for me. Peggy's dad was the vice principal of the junior high, and we had met in the creek on her first day in town about six weeks before. Now we met each Saturday for a special reason.

I would wade into the middle of the creek, and there, under a pile of rocks, I would get out the mason jar that contained the cigarettes we had taken from our dads. Then I walked up the slope by the bridge where we entered the bushes, which grew in such a way that they left a tunnel in the middle. There, we would sit and talk while smoking like locomotives until it was time for me to put the mason jar back under the pile of rocks so I could walk to the father's house for my Latin lessons.

Hey, Batter-Batter!

A week before summer vacation, I finished my Latin lessons, and now, on the last day of school, all I could do was daydream about all I was going to do.

The next day, as we finished breakfast, Dad left for work as he was on the day shift now, and as he walked out the front door, he called back to us, reminding us to do our chores and clean the yard. Having finished with breakfast, out we went, first to the woodpile, and as Key-Key collected kindling, Ronnie carried in the wood as I continued to chop wood. With the two of them cooperating, which had never happened before, we finished raking the yard, cutting the grass, and cleaning the pond in no time at all. Ronnie and Key-Key went in to get something to play with, and I went to the coal shed with the two big coal buckets to fill them and take them to the back porch before I was able to enjoy myself. Having finished, I went out to the front of the house, where I found Ronnie and Key-Key playing baseball and realizing the danger of playing in front of the big picture window. Instead of yelling at them, I asked them to play in the vacant lot next to the house. Surprisingly, Key-Key said okay as he threw the hardball to me and said, "Just pitch one, and then we will go over there." Well, Key-Key had never been able to come close to the ball before, let alone hit it. I was so convinced that he would never hit it, I began winding up and released the ball slowly to him.

I saw the bat meeting the ball, and my heart jumped up into my throat as Key-Key ran the bases, not realizing he had just made a forty-eight-dollar home run, as the ball crashed dead center into the big picture window, cracking the glass in every direction.

Like always, I took off running with my throat pounding since that is where my heart was. Running at full speed ahead, not knowing where I was going, leaving Ronnie and Key-Key to face Mom. About the time I was reaching the back of the house, I heard Key-Key say, "George did it." Oh no, what was I going to do now? Mom would never believe me since Key-Key was Mom and Dad's pet. At least that was the way I saw it because he never got spanked, not even when he hit Mom in the center of the forehead with the handle of a toy rifle. Back then, they were made of metal and not plastic, all because she was asleep in the chair and didn't pay attention to him.

I ran down the alley, up many streets, and up the hill until I could run no further and just kept on walking. I must have walked for miles until I found myself near my hideout up on the hill above the CF&I irrigation ditch. There I knew I could live for the rest of my life.

Well, I could have lived the rest of my life there, but I had forgotten that I ate three times a day, and I had no food there. My stomach began to growl as I heard Ronnie calling my name. It wasn't long before he poked his head into the hideout, telling me that everything was okay at home and that Dad was not mad. I just could not believe that Dad was not mad because he had every reason to be, and I had sure made myself look guilty. I told Ronnie to go home, but he would not budge. Then he began to tell me what was for supper, and that was all I needed to get me moving.

As each step brought us closer to home, I could just see Dad waiting for me with the belt in hand, and still, my stomach won out. I just kept thinking that I would be sore for a day or two, but my stomach would be full. I didn't mind getting the belt; it's just that this time I was innocent, but yet I was guilty in Dad's eyes because I was the oldest, and I was to set the example, and I knew better.

In the door, Ronnie and I went, and to my extreme surprise, everyone was at the table. We were told to sit down, and the blessing was said. Dad didn't say a word as he sat across me next to the wood and coal stove. To my right was Ipa, and to my left was Ronnie.

Have you ever noticed how quiet and still everything is just before a storm? Well, that is how the kitchen was that night.

Under the Table

The kitchen was silent and eerie that night as we sat there at supper. The food began to be passed around the table, and it finally came around to me. I loaded up my plate with some of everything, until it almost overflowed, for I was so hungry. Ipa began to harp at me for putting so much on my plate, and I just told her to stuff it quietly as Dad was on the other side. Pain entered my mind as it told me that Ipa had kicked me under the table, and for no reason. Without realizing it, my right hand had made a fist and punched Ipa on her left arm.

Dad had been controlling himself so well that when I punched Ipa, he must have thought that I was possessed by the devil, to just turn and punch my sister for no reason at all. His left arm moved so quickly and came pointing at me in such a flash that I was very lucky to notice that his hand had the poker in it. My quick reflexes told me to get under the table, and I automatically slid faster than any snake. Then I heard the poker hit the high back of the wooden chair. There under the table, I just shook with fright and was so scared I could not move. Meanwhile, Mom and Dad were arguing, as I was thanking my lucky stars for not being hit with that poker. Then Dad told me to get back in my chair, and I had best eat everything, or else I would really get it for wasting food. As Dad kept telling me to get out from under the table, I tried, I really did, but I just could not move until I saw his chair start sliding out.

I got up into my chair, and as Dad left the kitchen, he gave me that special look of his that told me I was really treading on thin ice. The food was cold. My hunger had gone, tears rolled down my face, though I was not crying, and I knew I had to eat everything even if it made me sick. I got the first mouthful down, and with each succeeding mouthful, I made up my mind that if I was to live to see twelve, I had to run away. That was it. I would run away, and no one would ever find me again.

Sailor Hat

One year had passed, and the thought of running away never did go further than thought, for here it was Saturday, June 8, when at six in the morning, Dad came into the room, waking all of us kids up, telling us to get dressed and hurry downstairs to eat breakfast, or we would do our work around the house and go without eating if we weren't seated at the table in fifteen minutes. One thing for sure, Dad never said something he didn't mean, so out of our beds we flew, getting dressed and running to the only bathroom in the house.

Everyone made it to the table with time to spare, and I think the last two never used soap to clean up with, but anyway, Mom began to dish up our eggs, potatoes, and bacon, and as we ate, Dad began handing out assignments to each of us, and once everyone had finished their jobs, then we could do almost anything we wanted for the rest of the day.

Ipa had to help Mom with the laundry. Ronnie had to rake the left side of the house. Key-Key just had to rake the area under the cherry trees, which was about half the length of the house on the right side. Kenny had to take in wood chips and fill up the small box by the big metal box where the chopped wood had to be laid in neatly and stacked about three feet above the box, which I had to fill, plus bring in two big buckets of coal and water the garden.

Breakfast was over, and as I walked outside to begin, the sun was out, and the sky did not have a cloud in it. The birds were singing, and the air was so clean and crisp, and the morning was already warm that one just had to take a deep breath to fill his lungs. Closing your eyes, one could smell the meadow in the mountains and almost hear the rush of water in a stream.

What a beautiful day. I could go on a hike to Rockville and see my godparents or go fishing, but before I made up my mind, I had plenty to do, and if I didn't get started, I wouldn't be able to do whatever I decided to do.

I headed for the woodpile, which was on the other side of the garage, and about halfway there, I turned on the valve that let the ditch water from the top of the hill rush into the ditch at the garden. Then I went to the garage and got the big flat shovel to use as a water stop in the ditch and went to the far end of the garden and opened up a few rows so that as soon as the water arrived, they would be watered. Then I went back to the woodpile and began chopping wood with all the pieces about the same size, throwing them into a pile.

To take a break from chopping the wood as soon as I had a medium-sized pile, I would carry in three or four armloads and stack it neatly in the big metal box. Then I would check to make sure that each garden row was completely watered, and if they were, I would open up a few more and move the big flat shovel near the rows that were to be watered, and then I went back to chopping wood.

Everything was going really good. The metal box was full of wood, the coal was taken in, and more than half of the garden had been watered, and all that was left was from the snowball tree to where the garden began, and that would only take maybe thirty minutes. Standing there watering the garden, I looked over to the front porch and saw that Ronnie was almost done. But Key-Key just sat there with his feet hanging off the front porch, staring up into the cherry trees. I guess he must have been daydreaming, seeing himself up in the tree with all the cherries ripe and juicy and he just eating every cherry he could reach until he became sick because when I walked up to him, I scared him.

Key-Key was holding the rake in front of him with both hands when I reached for it and told him that if all he was going to do was sit there, I would rake the yard so I could do as I wanted after I finished watering the garden. But Key-Key, being as hardheaded as a mule, wasn't about to do what I told him, even if it meant that I did his job for him. So I pulled on the rake to take it from him, but he held on to it. Then again, I pulled on it. Again and again, he pulled back on it, and I just could not resist, so I let go really quick, and with the force he was pulling, the rake handle came back at him, hitting him right on his nose and forehead, and all I could do was laugh as he began crying and hollering for Dad.

Dad must have been at the door because he was there so quickly. Key-Key explained exactly what happened in six words. "George hit me with the rake."

My mind sent signals to my feet, saying, *Run, George, run, you don't stand a chance*, and that was exactly what I did. I spun around and began running under the cherry trees toward the garden, as Dad yelled for me to stop, but my feet were going so fast it was hard for my body to keep up with them, let alone stop. Reaching the garden at a point near the snowball tree, I sensed something fly by when all at once, I was covered with snowball petals as they went flying all over me and the garden. I never did see the rake come flying, but that was what I sensed fly by, and as it hit the snowball tree, it had sent the snowball petals all over.

I continued running on the edge of the ditch, making sure I didn't step on any plants, and all I knew was that I was not going to stop, and when I reached the woodpile and had to jump to the right to keep from having the big flat shovel hit my foot after having bounced off the woodpile. That was when I realized that someone was really trying to stop me for good, and I was sure it had to be Dad. All at once, my eyes focused on the axe, and as I tried to speed up more, all I could think was, *Legs, don't fail me now*.

Across the alley and over the first set of tracks I went, jumping completely across the second set of tracks, and as my left foot hit the ground, I heard the clang of the axe hit the first rail of the second set of tracks. Down the alley, I ran as if going to town, and my legs didn't begin to slow down until I had gone two and a half blocks. I looked back just to make sure I was not being chased before I started walking. I reached up to my forehead to wipe off the sweat, only to realize I had been so scared I had forgotten to sweat. That was when

I noticed I still had my sailor cap on my head, and as I pulled it off my head, the rest of the snowball petals fell to the ground. Reaching the end of the third block, my mind began to play tricks on me by saying, *Shame on you, George. Running away like a coward instead of standing there like a man. Yeah*, I thought, *but you don't know my dad*, and again it began, *Are you going to be a man or a mouse?*

Well, I wanted to be a man, but at that moment, I felt being a mouse was the better part of valor. Over and over, I wrestled with my mind, only to agree that I was to turn around and go, face Dad, man to man. My mind was willing, but my feet refused to turn me around until I had reached the end of the fourth block by the fire station, where I crossed the tracks and decided to walk straight home on the sidewalk, even if I had to walk seven blocks going by way of the sidewalk. Well, I started the long walk home, and even my mind agreed that I just wanted to live a little longer before I met Dad man to man.

Slower, a person could not walk because it took me almost two hours to get to the block our house was on. Half a block from the house, and now my heart pounded so loud, I could hear it. My palms were sweating, and I kept swallowing, trying to get the lump out of my throat.

Dad was in the front yard, picking up some trash piles with the big flat shovel, and as he put a shovel full into the wheelbarrow, he saw me coming up the walk and began walking toward me with the shovel still in his right hand. I had to muster all the courage I had to keep from freezing where I was and to keep from running again as I continued to walk toward him, not knowing what to expect.

As we met, not a word was spoken, and I just continued walking because I did not know what else to do. Now as we walked, I was a step ahead of Dad and to his right, not exchanging a word. All I kept repeating to myself over and over was, "Act like a man." We were now at the edge of the garden, and since nothing was being said or done, all I could figure was that Dad was just waiting to get me into the house. But if that was the plan, I was going to go through with it, like a man. I would take my punishment and not shed a tear. As we neared the front gate to the house, I was so scared and yet so proud of myself when all at once, I glanced down and noticed that my shoelace was untied, and almost as fast, I dropped to one knee and bent over to tie my shoe. Just then, I felt a gust of wind go up my back and over my head, knocking my sailor cap off my head.

With my sudden movement to tie my shoe, Dad must have thought that I was going to take off like a streak of lightning again, for I had not realized that the gust of wind that had gone up my back and caused my sailor cap to fly off my head was caused by the shovel, as Dad apparently wanted to get in at least one good swat if I was taking off. But when that shovel hit the iron fence with a loud clang, I realized how close it had been to knocking my head off my shoulders, for it did knock off my sailor hat.

Driftwood

The sun promised to give us a hot day that Wednesday when Ronnie and I decided to go swimming at the river after we finished our chores, and for months, we both had gotten smart in not having Key-Key hanging around, for he would always tell on us.

We had been learning all the bends and turns of the river all the way from old lady Lippi's farm, down past Castle Hill, to Lobach's pond and beyond, for months now. The year before, we had taken seven old railroad ties from a pile where ties had been replaced at the bridge over the creek by our house. We had managed to float and drag them all the way down the creek to the river and then up to Lobach's pond where we made a raft out of them.

We made it to the river in no time after we had finished our chores, and I had with me some matches so I could smoke driftwood just like Huckleberry Finn. Off to Lobach's pond, we went to play on the raft. Soon the sun was up, and it was really getting hot. So we decided to go back down to where the creek entered the river to go swimming in the pool that it created.

Halfway there were some big logs that lay on the sand in the shape of a letter V. There, we decided to get undressed and see who could get to the pond first. Taking off our clothes and throwing them here and there over the logs, once completely undressed, we began running over the hot sand to the pond in our birthday suits.

Ronnie beat me to the pond, and he had gone into the area by the river where the sand seemed to act like quicksand, and all I could do was think, *How am I going to explain how and why he died?* So I went over to where he was, and while I was holding a long stick out to him, he grabbed hold of it, and I pulled him out. We continued to swim in the pond and later decided to jump into the current of the river and go down the river about a quarter of a mile, where we would get out and run back up to the pool.

After doing this about six times, as I was getting out of the river, Ronnie was standing there and was pointing upriver as he told me, "Look, there is a fire up there." All at once, we both realized at the same time that up there was where we had left all our clothes. In a dead run, we went, arriving there, and began to throw sand on the fire. Finally, we got the fire out, only to realize that the fire had started when some of the matches had fallen out of my pocket, and now all our clothes were ashes, except for the soles of Ronnie's new shoes. Needless to say, that was the end of swimming for that day.

The big question now was how we were going to get home without being seen. There still were a couple of pieces of elastic from our underwear that I used to tie Ronnie's soles to his feet, but I would just have to go barefooted, not to mention that sumo wrestlers wore more clothing than we had on.

We began our perilous journey up the creek that ran alongside Emerson Grade School, and the closer we got to the main highway, the more dodging and darting into the prickly bushes we had to do whenever we saw someone come near the creek.

Finally, we had made it past the main highway, the road that went to the grade school, and now we were at the railroad bridge, which was about two blocks from the house.

I tried and tried to get Ronnie to go home and bring me back some clothes, but he was so afraid of being caught that all he did was cry. Well, we could have stayed there until that night, but everyone came and played there all day long, and we had just been lucky that no one was there now. With only one thing to do, we made our way up to the railroad tracks and began running as fast as possible, only to get halfway home as the two o'clock passenger train came by. We were too far now to try and hide, and it seemed as if a million eyes were upon us. In the back gate, we ran, and oh what a stroke of luck because Mom had washed clothes, and there on the line were our pants and shirts. Immediately we grabbed a pair of pants and a shirt, and into the coal shed, we went to get dressed.

As we came out of the coal shed all dressed and barefooted, Dad came out of the garage. I was caught dead to rights. There were no excuses now, as Dad found out what had happened from Ronnie and let me have it good. We were placed on restriction from going beyond the main highway, and that ensured we would not be able to get anywhere near the river. Now we would just start exploring the hills.

Tabletop

Little did we realize at that time that exploring the hills would be so interesting and that all our free time for the rest of the year would be spent learning each part of the hills better than the prairie dogs. We explored the area about fifteen miles south of Florence, where we could find arrowheads on the other side of the road that went to Wetmore. Then all the area around the house that was made of two railroad cabooses, where we met a really nice lady who always had lemonade and a snack whenever we were around. We must have been inside every abandoned mine shaft, and the only place that I never liked was the bat cave near Coaldale. Whenever we had any money and were in that area, we would go into the only grocery store in Coaldale and get Coke. It was directly across what used to be a jail, which still had bars on the door and window and was only about eight feet square.

On Saturdays, we would always go to Rockville, where my godmother lived because she would pack a lunch, and we would climb the biggest hill around, which was called tabletop, and would start a small fire to roast hot dogs and marshmallows, plus eat all the other food that she packed into the picnic basket.

My godmother was something else because she would play ball with us and hike, and she always cooked something for us. In fact, I remember one Saturday morning when I arrived early and both my godmother and godfather were eating breakfast. I was immediately asked to sit down and have some pancakes and eggs with bacon. The reason it stands out is that to this day, I still place my eggs between the pancakes like a sandwich before pouring on the syrup.

Raton

I was in high school now, and only one week remained until summer vacation when Dad told me that this summer, I was going to Raton to help my brother Andy in his shoe shop.

All week long, I wondered what Raton would be like and what I would be doing in the shoe shop, and yet I couldn't help but wonder how much my dad had paid Andy to keep me for the summer break.

Well, school was out, and almost as fast, Dad had the car loaded, and we headed off to Raton, New Mexico. Once we arrived, I stayed with Andy at the shoe shop until Bennie, my other brother who was a railroad telegrapher, got off duty. Bennie came over to the shop, picked me and my clothes up, and took me home with him because I was going to be staying with Cora's mother, Doña Emilia, who lived across the street from Bennie and Cora. Cora was such a beautiful lady, and I still remember being at their wedding where I was the ring bearer in my sailor suit.

The next day came early as Bennie and I left after breakfast, him to go to work and me to the shoe shop. The shoe shop had two distinct odors: one was the horse glue used to stick on the sole of the shoe, and the other was sawdust. I soon got so used to the smell that I didn't notice it. Andy began to show me around the shop, all the machinery that was used, and how to use it. Then he introduced me to Jimmie Ortega, who had worked for Andy last year during the school break and was also going to work during the school break this year.

My first week was spent ripping off the heels and soles of every pair of shoes and boots in Raton. When I wasn't ripping things apart,

I was shining shoes and boots. Jimmie only lived about five blocks further up the hill from where I was staying, and he walked to work each day. After church on Sunday, I went over to Jimmie's house, and that was when I found out that he had eleven brothers and sisters, and boy was their dining room table long. We went on a hike up the hill, and he was telling me about all the things I still had to learn at the shop, everything from how to dye and stretch shoes to running the sanding machines that ground off the excess leather and rubber off the shoes, to the monster machine that stitched on the leather soles. Then he began to tell me how nicely Andy treated him and that Andy had a gorgeous babysitter whose name was Lucy.

Time went by fast each week with me trying to learn all the different machinery. Andy was sanding the leather heel on a pair of boots when a customer came in, and he handed the boot to me to finish. While he was busy, I began to sand the heel when all at once, it slipped out of my hands and got stuck in the sander. The machine kept running and running until the boot started to smoke, and Andy rushed over and hit the emergency stop. Andy turned without saying a word and went and finished talking to the customer. He came back, took the boot out of the sander, and when another customer came in wanting a shoeshine, he asked me to go give him a shoeshine while he worked on the boot.

You know, Andy never did say anything about the boot I had put a quarter-sized hole in but showed me again how to hold onto a shoe so it would not slip out of my hands. About a week later, the owner of the boot with the quarter-sized hole in it came to pick it up. Andy had done such a good job fixing the hole that the man did not notice where it had happened until Andy showed him where it was. He also told him that he had done it, apologized, and said there was no charge. In fact, he gave him a brand-new pair of boots. The man wanted to refuse both offers, saying that accidents do happen, but Andy would not let him.

I used to eat most of my meals with Doña Emilia and at Bennie's, and the best meal of all was when Cora would make liver and onions. How she prepared it, I don't know, but it sure was delicious, with each slice of liver being so thin.

Often, I would walk over to Andy's and Fabbie's house on the weekends, and Lucy would try to teach me how to jitterbug until I think she realized that I had two left feet. But I always stayed for dinner, and Lucy and I would take a walk so we could smoke our cigarettes—her with her non-filtered Lucky Strikes and me with my filtered Winstons. We would talk about almost anything, and I would tell her about Jimmie and how badly he wanted to date her but was too afraid to ask her. Then she would try and convince me to go out with Proxie, who belonged to a gang of girls and lived next to Andy.

Finally, one week later, Andy gave Jimmie and me a Saturday off. I don't know if it happened by chance or if he knew that we had made plans to go on a picnic and to the afternoon movie with Lucy and Dorothy. When we picked up the girls, I introduced Jimmie to Lucy, my niece, and we headed off to the hills for our picnic. Jimmie was a little taller than Lucy, and Dorothy was about six inches taller than me since I was only four feet eleven and weighed less than one hundred pounds. As it would happen, when we got to the theater, some of the local boys began making fun of me and Dorothy. Then out of nowhere, Proxie showed up and put them in their place, and the rest of the day was just wonderful. I'll bet that Lucy told Andy what had happened because, after that, whenever I went over to Andy's, he would tease me about how much Proxie liked me.

July 4 was coming, and Andy told me that we would be going to the ranch early Friday morning and would not be back until Monday. I was to gather some of my clothes and spend the night at Andy's because, just like Dad, we had to be on the road in the cool of the morning.

That Thursday night, we sat at the kitchen table, and I found out that this other girl, whose name was Gigi, was also going with us to the ranch because her mom and dad also lived there. I never knew why she was in Raton. With supper over and Andy wanting to be on the road before six in the morning, we went to bed early—the girls in the living room and me in the kitchen.

At four-thirty in the morning, there at the foot of my makeshift bed on the floor were Gigi and Lucy, as they both grabbed the blanket at my feet. Gigi said, "I wonder if he sleeps in his underwear."

Then the tug of war began with the blanket until Andy hollered, "What's going on in there?" The girls took off back into the living room, and I went ahead and got up.

After breakfast and dishes were done, we loaded up the car and were on the highway heading for the ranch. Now Andy's car—I don't remember what kind it was—did have a front and back seat and was big enough for six people, but once everyone was in, I realized why they called them coupes: because with six in that car, you were really cooped up.

Andy, Fabbie, and the baby were in front, with me stuck in the middle between Lucy on my right and Gigi on my left. After miles on the road and Andy having watched me getting poked, prodded, pinched, and tickled on both sides by Lucy and Gigi, he finally figured out a way to have them stop without telling them.

That was when Andy said that he knew that we smoked and that we could smoke. For Lucy's sake, he said he would not tell Lola, her mom. The cigarettes came out in a flash, and all the windows came down, which made the car air-conditioned. That was how cars had air-conditioning then: all windows down and speeding down Highway 25 at seventy-five miles an hour. I began to make smoke rings and soon finished my cigarette and threw it out the window. Then the girls wanted to learn how to make the smoke rings, so we each lit another cigarette and began blowing smoke rings at the back of Andy's and Fabbie's heads. I finished mine and threw the cigarette out the front window by Fabbie, and we must have gone about twenty miles when Lucy began to say that the car was on fire. Little did I know that when I threw out my cigarette, it had come back in through the back window and landed on the seat next to Lucy. The car came to a stop on the side of the road, and Andy got the water to put out the fire. I don't know. With the fire out, we headed on to the ranch. Needless to say, we did not smoke in the car anymore.

The Ranch

You have heard of "over the river and through the woods." Well, let me tell you how to get to the ranch.

Once you left Las Vegas heading south for about four miles, you came to Romeroville, where Don Pantaleon had a small grocery store and gas station. From there, you went about eight more miles, then you got off Highway 25 on a small road that you entered between a fence that came to the edge of the cattle guard. The road must have been paved about thirty years before because grass and weeds grew through it all over the place. However, it was only paved through the town of Bernal because, at the top of the hill, the pavement stopped, and the dusty cow trail began.

Another cattle guard, and I swear, this road was made by two cows walking side by side. Every two feet, there was a hole on one side or the other, and the piñon trees at each bend in the trail reached out and scratched the car. Down the hill we went, bouncing up and down and side to side until you got to the river that went over the road.

Through the river, we went, up the hill to Chappell, where Andy and his brothers and sisters had been born and also where Dad had grown up and herded goats on the hills up above and behind their house, and where, before he died, my grandpa had a general store. We turned right out of Chappell and another cattle guard, and now for the worst part of the cow trail, holes so big, they seemed to swallow Andy's car, but we finally got to the ranch.

Turning left off the road, we entered the yard at the ranch. The main house was made of sandstone rock, and to the right of the house was a long building that had about six apartments, plus what at one time was a post office and grocery store. This building was also made of large sandstone rock and mud. Attached sideways to this building was a big garage that housed the truck, tractor, and car. Out of the car and into the house we went, and straight to the kitchen table because no matter what time of day or night you got to the ranch, you had to sit down and eat. Everything was put away, and I went outside with Tomas and David to play ball.

The next morning, I helped Tomas and David with their chores before we headed out across the road to the makeshift baseball field and golf course as we headed toward Starvation Peak, checking on the cows and making sure I did not step on a fresh pile of manure. Why we had brought the gunny sacks with us, I did not know. We walked and walked, and on our return, Tomas decided to go swimming in the creek. We climbed down into the creek, which had no water running in it, to a pool of water. There we stripped down to our shorts, and Tomas was the first to jump in with his mouth wide open, coming up spitting water out. David and I were swimming around when I kept feeling slime on every part of my body that was underwater. I reached down into the water, cupped my hands, and brought up a handful of water with so many tadpoles that I had more tadpoles in my hand than water. Surely each time Tomas went under the water with his mouth open, he must have got some in his mouth. I got out of the pool and sat on a rock until my shorts were dry, and then got dressed.

Tomas and David had gotten out of the water shortly after I did and were all dressed now as we began to head back to the ranch. Now I found out that we were to fill our gunny sacks with dry cow chips so that we could burn them outside at night when the fireworks were set off, and that way, we would not be pestered by the mosquitoes.

That Sunday morning, after church and chores were done, Tomas and David went out and caught the horses as I watched. They put on the bridles, and handing me the reins to one of the horses, Tomas mounted his palomino. He pulled back on the reins, and his horse stood on its hind legs before he took it for a short run. Now his palomino was a very big horse, and when he just rode him or even at a slow gallop, the horse kept his head straight. But let him take off in a dead run, and that horse turned his head all the way to the left so much so that one eye was on the rider and the other straight ahead. Tomas got off his horse, and we walked them to the cistern to water them before we went for a ride.

The horses watered, and all three of us mounted bareback on the horses. Lola came out and told them to take care of me since it was my first time on a horse. Tomas looked at David, and both promised their mother they would take care of me, but I just wondered why they each had a grin on their face.

Out of the yard and up the road toward Chappell we went at a slow pace, just talking about almost anything. We made it to Chappell, turned around at the railroad tracks, and headed back to the ranch. Everything was going really well until we got to about a mile from the ranch when Tomas decided to race to the ranch.

He reached over, swatted my horse on the hind end, let out a yell so loud my horse reared up on its hind legs, did a right turn, and headed across the road. It jumped the small fence and just kept running through the scrub and piñon trees so fast that I was riding the horse sideways, first to the left, then to the right, and trying to keep from being hit by the piñon branches, for I was hanging on for dear life. The horse finally came to a dead stop at the edge of the ravine, with my stomach at the horse's ears, my arms around his head in a choke hold, and my eyes wide open, staring down into the deep ravine. That was how Tommie and David found us a few minutes later. After my horse was able to breathe again, we headed back to the ranch.

Morning came, and we were all packed and ready to head back to Raton when I asked Andy if Gigi was going back also, and to my relief, he told me no. On the way back, we went past Springer when all at once, I looked down only to let out a big scream, as on my lap was a snake. I hit it with my right hand and knocked it to the floor by Lucy's feet. Now Fabbie was screaming, and as Andy pulled off the road, Lucy bent over, picked up the garter snake, took it out of the car, and let it go. Andy was laughing so hard, and Lucy kept stifling her laughter. As for me, I realized that Fabbie hated snakes as much as I did, and for some reason, I never did blame Lucy but thought that this was something that Gigi had talked Lucy into doing.

Bribes

Back in Raton, I kept busy, and one morning, while I was giving a man a shoeshine, he asked me if I was out of high school yet. I told him I would graduate next year, and then he told me that I could make a lot of money if I became a jockey and that he was willing to train me. I immediately responded, "No, thank you." I never told him why not, but as for me, I knew how lucky I was to have survived my stay at the ranch.

Time went by so fast, and to my surprise, Dad had come for me early. I often wondered if Andy had told Dad that I had burned his car, or if he had paid Dad twice as much to take me home early.

Back in Florence, I finished that summer working on the different farms in the area. I had been working at the farms on weekends before graduation when I found out that Ambrose had been talking to the army recruiter and was about to join up.

I found myself deciding to go into the air force upon graduation, only to be rejected because I only weighed ninety-eight pounds and was only four feet eleven inches tall. I did not want to go into the army, so I talked to the navy recruiter and was ready to have Dad sign the papers when the recruiter would return in two weeks.

Eight days before the navy recruiter was due to return, I went to see Ambrose at the malt shop, which was where the bus station was, before he left for the army because he had enlisted to jump out of perfectly good airplanes.

There at the malt shop, I saw Ambrose, who was all set to go, and my aunt sitting beside him with tears in her eyes. Ambrose saw me and almost immediately had the army recruiter pounce on me.

After the recruiter was convinced by everyone in the malt shop that I had indeed graduated from high school, he began to bribe me with hamburgers and milkshakes.

The recruiter definitely did his job because, by Monday, I had gone through all the boxes of papers that Mom kept in the closet to find the names and addresses of all my relatives. That was when I found out that Dad had worked for the railroad when I was born, and at that time, we lived in a boxcar that had been made into a home. I was born at the Benston station, near Timpas, Colorado. At that time, Dad traveled all over Colorado and New Mexico repairing the railroad tracks.

I had been to Denver, where I ate five pounds of bananas to make the weight and stood on my tiptoes to make the height, and now I was at the malt shop waiting for the bus to arrive.

Everything was fine, except for Ipa, who was crying. As the bus came down the street, everyone who was there began saying their goodbyes, as Ipa cried louder. The bus came to a stop, and as everyone began to line up to board, the bus driver began to collect tickets. I knelt before Dad, with watering eyes, and he began to give me his blessing in Spanish, saying as he made the sign of the cross over me, "May Almighty God walk before you, beside you, and behind you. May He also make each of your burdens light and each byway straight. May your days be filled with happiness and your children fill your heart with gladness as you have mine. Foremost, my son, I love you. May Almighty God bless you and keep you in the name of the Father, Son, and Holy Spirit, Amen."

As he finished making the sign of the cross over me once again, he placed his hand before me to kiss in acceptance of his blessing.

Getting up with tears rolling down my cheeks, I hugged and told Dad that I loved him, and then I hugged Mom and Ipa before boarding the bus to Denver again and on into the army.

About the Author

George Solano was born three years before the official end of World War II at a location known as Benton, located between La Junta and Walsenburg, Colorado. His recollection of the towns he was raised in is still vivid in his mind, and his description of Portland and Florence, Colorado, will transport you there to a time after World War II. As you read his compilation, you'll encounter hilarious episodes that occurred prior to his volunteering to enlist in the US Army.

Printed in the USA
CPSIA information can be obtained
at www.ICGtesting.com
CBHW021617270724
12235CB00008B/194